Bio

D1087887

Andrew Garfield

ABDO
Publishing Company

Big Buddy BOOKS
Buddy Bios

by **Sarah Tieck**

VISIT US AT
www.abdopublishing.com

Published by ABDO Publishing Company, PO Box 398166, Minneapolis, Minnesota 55439.

Printed in the United States of America, North Mankato, Minnesota.
102013
012014

 PRINTED ON RECYCLED PAPER

Coordinating Series Editor: Rochelle Baltzer
Contributing Editors: Megan M. Gunderson, Bridget O'Brien, Marcia Zappa
Graphic Design: Maria Hosley
Cover Photograph: *AP Photo*: Jon Furniss/Invision.
Interior Photographs/Illustrations: *AP Photo*: Matt Dunham (p. 13), Andrew Medichini (p. 11), Rex Features via
    AP Images (p. 5), Markus Schreiber (p. 5), Charles Sykes (p. 19), Charles Sykes/Invision (p. 19), Alexander
    Zemlianichenko (p. 24); *Getty Images*: Aby Baker (p. 23), Dave M. Benett (pp. 7, 9), Gregg DeGuire/FilmMagic
    (p. 17), Sean Gallup/Getty Images for Sony Pictures (p. 21), Jamie McCarthy/Getty Images for EIF Revlon Run
    Walk (p. 27), Jamie McCarthy/WireImage (p. 27), Jeff Vespa/WireImage (p. 15), Kevin Winter (p. 29).

Library of Congress Cataloging-in-Publication Data

Tieck, Sarah, 1976-
  Andrew Garfield : star of the amazing Spider-Man / Sarah Tieck.
    pages cm. -- (Big buddy biographies)
  ISBN 978-1-62403-198-4
1. Garfield, Andrew, 1983---Juvenile literature. 2. Actors--United States--Biography--Juvenile literature. I. Title.
  PN2287.G375T54 2014
  791.4302'8092--dc23
  [B]
                            2013031964

Andrew
Garfield

Contents

Screen Star

Andrew Garfield is a talented actor. He has appeared in several movies and television shows. He is famous for starring in *The Amazing Spider-Man*. He is also known for acting on stage in plays.

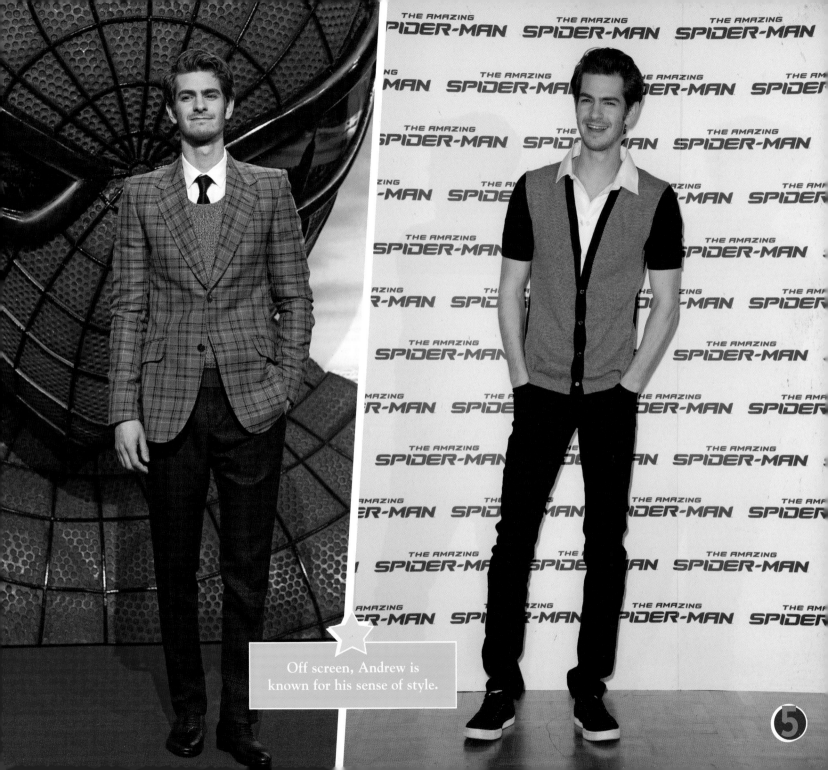

Off screen, Andrew is known for his sense of style.

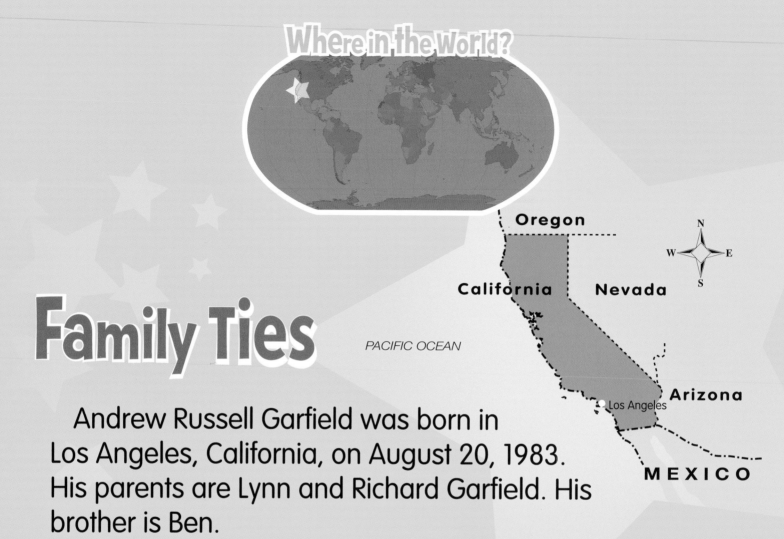

Oregon

California Nevada

PACIFIC OCEAN

Los Angeles

Arizona

MEXICO

Family Ties

Andrew Russell Garfield was born in Los Angeles, California, on August 20, 1983. His parents are Lynn and Richard Garfield. His brother is Ben.

Andrew's mother is British, and his father is American. When Andrew was about three, his family moved to England. There, his parents had an **interior design** business.

6

7

Did you know...

When Andrew was young, he practiced gymnastics.

Sometimes, Andrew's parents attend events with him.

Young Talent

Andrew grew up in Surrey, England. It is near London. There, Andrew became interested in acting. He trained to be an actor at London's Central School of Speech and Drama. He finished school in 2004.

In 2005, Andrew began acting **professionally**. He acted in plays, such as *Romeo and Juliet*. Also that year, he appeared on a television show called *Sugar Rush*.

In 2006, Andrew won the *Evening Standard* newspaper's Milton Shulman Award for Outstanding Newcomer. This was his first acting award.

Working Actor

Andrew was becoming known for his work. In 2007, he appeared in a movie called *Boy A*. In 2009, he appeared in a three-part television special called *Red Riding*.

Andrew's first **role** in an American movie came in 2007. The movie was called *Lions for Lambs*. He worked with well-known actors Meryl Streep and Robert Redford. People were impressed with Andrew's strong acting.

Andrew worked with Michael Peña, Robert Redford, and Tom Cruise (*left to right*) in *Lions for Lambs*. Robert is one of his acting heroes. So, he was especially excited to work with him.

Making Movies

After *Lions for Lambs*, Andrew began to get more movie **roles** and work in the United States. In 2009, he acted in *The Imaginarium of Doctor Parnassus*.

For this movie, Andrew worked with more famous actors. They included Heath Ledger, Johnny Depp, and Christopher Plummer. Andrew learned more about acting from working with them.

Andrew played a magician in *Doctor Parnassus*. He did stage magic called "sleight of hand."

In 2010, Andrew starred in *Never Let Me Go*. People noticed his skill in playing a young man named Tommy, who had a difficult life. Soon, Andrew would have more opportunities. Each part helped him grow as an actor.

Andrew's costar in *Never Let Me Go* was Carey Mulligan.

Big Break

In 2010, Andrew got a **role** in *The Social Network*. The movie was about the founding of Facebook. Andrew played the Web site's cofounder, Eduardo Saverin.

Andrew stood out as a talented actor. There were news stories about his acting. Also, he was **nominated** for a BAFTA Award. Then, *The Social Network* won three Academy Awards!

16

Andrew acted with Justin Timberlake and Jesse Eisenberg in *The Social Network*.

Stage Actor

Andrew started out as a stage actor. In 2012, he returned to the stage. He got a **role** in a **Broadway** play called *Death of a Salesman*.

The play is about salesman Willy Loman, who feels sad about his life. Andrew played Biff Loman, Willy's oldest child. He was **nominated** for a **Tony Award** for this role!

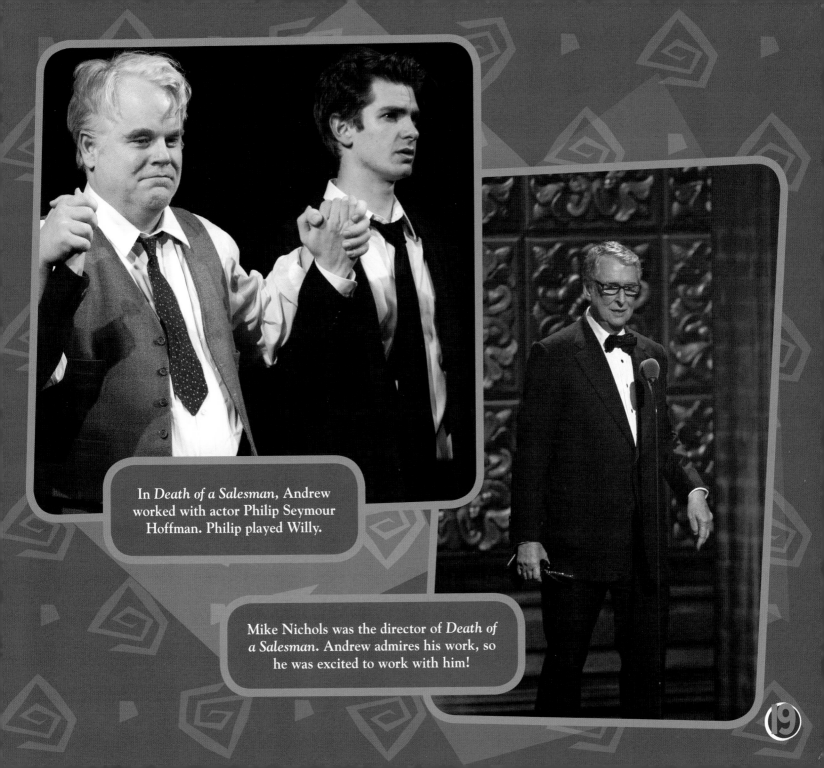

In *Death of a Salesman*, Andrew worked with actor Philip Seymour Hoffman. Philip played Willy.

Mike Nichols was the director of *Death of a Salesman*. Andrew admires his work, so he was excited to work with him!

Big Opportunities

In 2012, Andrew starred in *The Amazing Spider-Man*. This movie is about Peter Parker becoming Spider-Man. It is based on a comic book story.

Andrew was excited to be chosen to play Peter Parker. This was his first lead part in a big movie. Andrew also understood his character. He had been picked on by bigger kids while growing up.

An Actor's Life

As an actor, Andrew spends time practicing **lines** and **performing**. He may be on a movie **set** for many hours each day.

Some of this time is spent filming. And, some of it is spent getting ready. Actors and actresses put on makeup and wear special clothes to look like their characters.

In the Amazing Spider-Man movies, Andrew did some of his own stunts using special wires.

23

When Andrew attends events, he signs autographs and takes pictures with fans.

Sometimes, Andrew travels to make or **promote** his movies. He may be away from home for several days or even months. During this time, he talks to reporters about his upcoming **roles**. He also appears on television and radio shows.

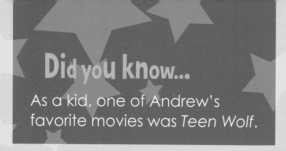

Did you know...

As a kid, one of Andrew's favorite movies was *Teen Wolf*.

Off the Screen

When Andrew is not working, he spends time with his family, friends, and dog. He enjoys being at home. He exercises and goes biking.

Andrew likes to help others. He has **volunteered** his time to help people, especially kids. Some groups he supports include the Boys and Girls Club and the Worldwide Orphans Foundation.

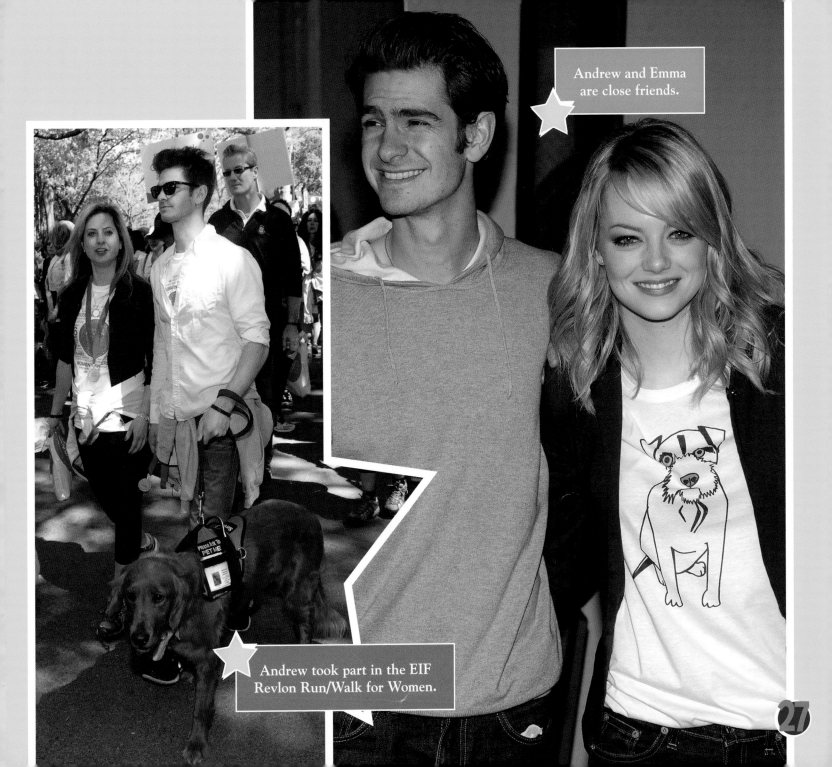

Andrew and Emma are close friends.

Andrew took part in the EIF Revlon Run/Walk for Women.

27

In 2013, Andrew spoke at Comic-Con International in San Diego, California. This event is popular with comic book fans.

Buzz

In 2014, Andrew returned to the **role** of Peter Parker in *The Amazing Spider-Man 2*. Andrew's fame continues to grow. Fans look forward to what's next for him! Many believe he has a bright **future**.

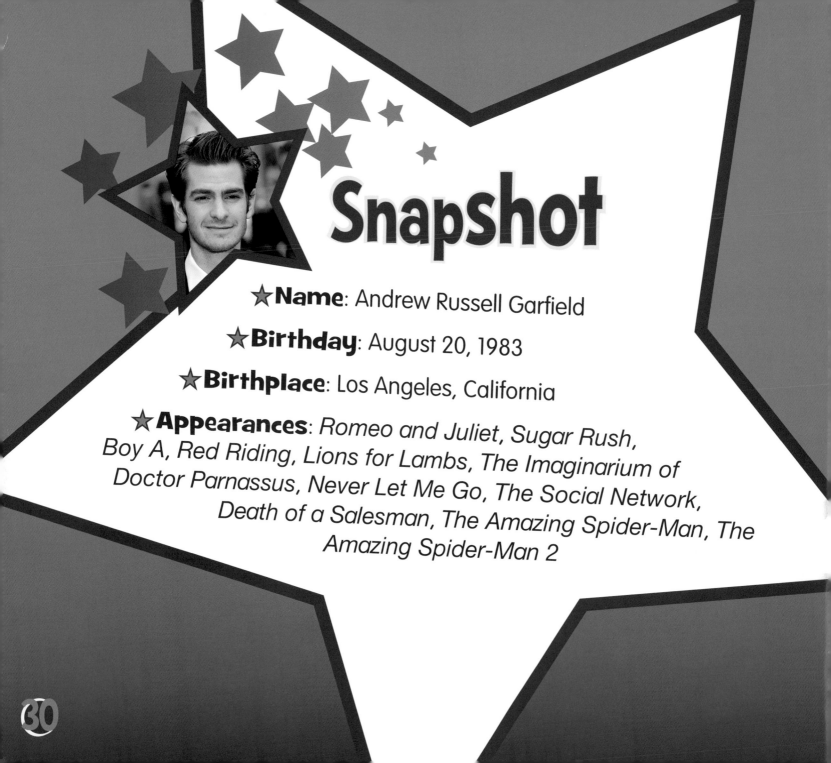

Snapshot

★**Name**: Andrew Russell Garfield

★**Birthday**: August 20, 1983

★**Birthplace**: Los Angeles, California

★**Appearances**: *Romeo and Juliet, Sugar Rush, Boy A, Red Riding, Lions for Lambs, The Imaginarium of Doctor Parnassus, Never Let Me Go, The Social Network, Death of a Salesman, The Amazing Spider-Man, The Amazing Spider-Man 2*

Important Words

Broadway a part of New York City, New York, famous for its theaters.

future (FYOO-chuhr) a time that has not yet occurred.

interior design (ihn-TIHR-ee-uhr dih-ZINE) the act or job of decorating the insides of buildings and homes.

lines the words an actor says in a play, a movie, or a show.

nominate to name as a possible winner.

perform to do something in front of an audience.

professional (pruh-FEHSH-nuhl) working for money rather than only for pleasure.

promote to help something become known.

role a part an actor plays.

set the place where a movie or a television show is recorded.

Tony Award an award that recognizes excellence in Broadway theater.

volunteer (vah-luhn-TIHR) to help others in one's free time without pay.

Web Sites

To learn more about Andrew Garfield, visit ABDO Publishing Company online. Web sites about Andrew Garfield are featured on our Book Links page. These links are routinely monitored and updated to provide the most current information available.

www.abdopublishing.com

Index